Title: Healing from Narcissistic Practical Guide

Table of Contents:

1. Introduction
    - Understanding Narcissistic Family Dynamics
    - The Impact on Individuals
2. Chapter 1: Recognizing Narcissistic Family Patterns
    - Identifying Narcissistic Behaviour
    - Common Roles and Dynamics
3. Chapter 2: Effects of Growing Up in a Narcissistic Family
    - Low Self-Esteem and Insecurity
    - Difficulty Setting Boundaries
    - Coping Mechanisms and Their Consequences
4. Chapter 3: Healing the Self
    - Cultivating Self-Awareness
    - Rebuilding Self-Esteem
    - Reclaiming Your Identity
5. Chapter 4: Setting Healthy Boundaries
    - Understanding Personal Boundaries
    - Strategies for Implementing Boundaries
    - Navigating Pushback and Resistance
6. Chapter 5: Communication and Relationships

- Learning Healthy Communication
- Strategies for Assertive Communication
- Nurturing Supportive Relationships

7. **Chapter 6: Coping with Emotional Challenges**
    - Managing Anxiety and Depression
    - Developing Emotional Resilience
    - Practicing Self-Care

8. **Chapter 7: Strategies for Healing**
    - Seeking Professional Help
    - Mindfulness and Meditation
    - Creative Expression as Therapy

9. **Chapter 8: Practical Steps for Building a Stronger Self**
    - Affirmations for Positive Self-Beliefs
    - Journaling Prompts for Self-Reflection
    - Implementing Healthy Daily Routines

10. **Chapter 9: Case Studies and Real-Life Examples**
    - Profiles of Individuals and Their Healing Journeys
    - Practical Examples of Boundary Setting, Communication, and Self-Care

11. **Chapter 10: Moving Forward and Thriving**
    - Celebrating Progress

- Long-Term Strategies for Continued Growth
- Creating a Supportive Network

12. Conclusion
- Embracing Healing as a Continuous Journey
- Empowering Yourself to Break Cycles

From the shadows of narcissistic family dynamics, we emerge not as victims, but as survivors with the power to rewrite our own stories of resilience, healing, and triumphant self-discovery.

Though the scars of narcissistic family dynamics may run deep, they do not define us. We have the power to mend, grow, and thrive, revealing the resilient and vibrant individuals we were always meant to be.

Preface

In the tapestry of life, family is often our first and most profound connection. It's within the family unit that we learn to love, to trust, and to grow. But what happens when this unit is marred by the presence of narcissistic traits or personalities? How do we navigate the complex web of emotions, expectations, and roles when one family member's need for attention and admiration takes centre stage?

This eBook is a journey through the intricate landscape of narcissistic family dynamics. It's a journey of understanding, healing, and transformation. It's a journey for those who have found themselves entangled in a family where narcissism casts a long shadow.

Within these pages, we will explore the roles family members often adopt in response to the narcissistic figure's dominance. We will delve into the effects of growing up in such an environment, from low self-esteem to difficulty setting boundaries. But we won't stop there. This eBook is not just about understanding; it's about empowerment.

Through real-life anecdotes, detailed explanations, practical exercises, and actionable advice, we will embark on a path to healing. We will learn how to cultivate self-awareness, rebuild self-esteem, and reclaim our identity. We will explore the art of setting healthy boundaries, communicating effectively, and nurturing supportive relationships outside the family.

We will discover how to cope with emotional challenges, managing anxiety and depression, and practicing self-care. And we will uncover strategies for healing that go beyond traditional therapy, including mindfulness, creative expression, and spiritual practices.

This journey is not one to be taken alone. It's a collective voyage toward healthier relationships and a stronger sense of self. It's a testament to the human spirit's resilience, the capacity to not just survive but to thrive.

If you've ever felt trapped in the shadow of a narcissistic family dynamic, know that you are not alone. You are part of a community of individuals who have faced similar challenges and emerged stronger. You have the power to rewrite your story, to break free from cycles that no longer serve you, and to create a life that aligns with your true self.

So, let's embark on this journey together—a journey of healing, empowerment, and transformation. Let's discover the path to not just surviving but thriving beyond narcissistic family dynamics.

Introduction

Narcissistic traits are a set of personality characteristics and behaviours associated with narcissism, a personality trait or disorder characterized by an excessive preoccupation with oneself, a need for constant attention and admiration, and a lack of empathy for others. It's important to note that having a few narcissistic traits doesn't necessarily mean a person has narcissistic personality disorder (NPD), which is a more severe and pervasive condition.

Here are some common narcissistic traits:

1. **Grandiosity:** A grandiose sense of self-importance, often exaggerating achievements and talents and expecting to be recognized as superior.

2. **Need for Admiration:** An insatiable desire for attention, praise, and admiration from others, often seeking constant validation.

3. **Lack of Empathy:** Difficulty or inability to understand or relate to the feelings and needs of others, leading to a lack of compassion.

4. **Entitlement:** Believing that one is inherently deserving of special treatment, privileges, and recognition without necessarily earning them.

5. **Exploitative Behaviour:** Taking advantage of others for personal gain, without regard for their well-being or feelings.

6. **Manipulation:** Using various tactics to control and manipulate others to achieve one's goals or maintain a sense of superiority.

7. **Difficulty Accepting Criticism:** Reacting negatively or defensively to criticism, often feeling attacked or insulted when confronted with even constructive feedback.

8. **Envy:** Feeling envious of others' success, often belittling, or downplaying their achievements to protect one's own ego.

9. **Arrogance:** Displaying a haughty attitude and an air of superiority, looking down upon those deemed as inferior.

10. **Boundary Violations:** Ignoring or disregarding others' boundaries and personal space, often invading their privacy or overstepping boundaries.

It's important to remember that while some level of self-confidence and self-interest is healthy, an excessive display of these traits can negatively impact relationships and well-being. Individuals with significant narcissistic traits may struggle with forming meaningful connections, empathy, and maintaining healthy interactions. If you suspect someone's narcissistic traits are causing significant distress or harm to themselves or others, professional help should be considered.

Growing up in a family should ideally provide a foundation of love, support, and nurturing. However, for those who have experienced narcissistic family dynamics, the reality can be far from this ideal. Narcissistic family dynamics are characterized by a central figure who seeks admiration, control, and validation at the expense of other family members' emotional well-being. This behaviour can manifest in parents, siblings, or even extended family members, leaving a lasting impact on individuals who grow up in such an environment.

Understanding Narcissistic Family Dynamics

At the core of narcissistic family dynamics is a skewed power structure. The narcissistic individual, often a parent or older sibling, dominates the family unit with their insatiable need for attention and affirmation. Their behaviour tends to revolve around their own desires and emotions, while the needs of others are pushed aside or ignored. The family members orbit around this central figure, often adopting roles that either align with or counteract the narcissist's behaviour.

Understanding Narcissistic Family Dynamics: Unravelling the Power Structure

Skewed Power Structure: At the heart of narcissistic family dynamics lies a complex power structure that shapes the interactions and relationships within the family unit. This structure is typically anchored by an individual with narcissistic traits or a full-blown narcissistic personality disorder. This individual, often a parent or older sibling, holds a disproportionate amount of influence and control.

Dominance and Attention: The narcissistic figure's presence is all-consuming, as they hunger for unceasing attention, admiration, and affirmation. Their behaviour revolves around their own desires, emotions, and ego, often relegating the needs and feelings of others to the background. This self-centred focus becomes the gravitational centre of the family's universe, distorting the natural balance of relationships.

Neglected Needs: Within this power structure, the needs and emotions of other family members can become secondary. As the narcissistic individual's demands take precedence, others' desires and well-being are frequently overshadowed or dismissed. The family dynamic perpetuates a cycle of catering to the narcissist's needs while suppressing the legitimate needs of other members.

Orbiting Roles: Family members, in response to the narcissistic figure's dominance, often adopt roles that either align with or counteract their behaviour. These roles become coping mechanisms and strategies to navigate the challenging environment.

The Impact on Individuals

The effects of growing up in a narcissistic family environment can be profound and enduring. Children who experience these dynamics can develop a range of emotional, psychological, and interpersonal challenges that extend into adulthood.

A sense of self-worth becomes linked to the approval of the narcissistic family member, leading to issues of low self-esteem, anxiety, and even depression.

The invalidation of emotions and the stifling of personal expression can hinder the development of healthy coping mechanisms, resulting in difficulties in handling stress and conflict.

An individual's ability to form and maintain relationships outside the family can also be hindered. Healthy boundaries, a cornerstone of balanced relationships, may be unclear or entirely absent in narcissistic family dynamics. This lack of boundary-setting can lead to issues such as co-dependency, difficulty saying no, and a tendency to prioritize the needs of others over one's own.

Growing up in a narcissistic family unit can have profound and lasting effects on individuals. The dynamics within such families can be emotionally manipulative, inconsistent, and damaging, leading to a range of psychological, emotional, and interpersonal challenges.

Here are some common effects that individuals who have been raised in narcissistic family units might experience:

1. **Low Self-Esteem:** Children in narcissistic families often receive inconsistent and conditional love. They might internalize the message that their worth is tied

to their ability to please the narcissistic family member, leading to low self-esteem and a lack of self-confidence.

2. **Lack of Boundaries:** Narcissistic family units tend to disregard personal boundaries. As a result, individuals who grow up in such environments might struggle to establish healthy boundaries in their relationships later in life, leading to difficulties in asserting their needs and protecting themselves.

3. **Co-dependency:** Children raised in narcissistic families often learn to prioritize the needs and emotions of others over their own. This can lead to codependent behaviours, where they become overly focused on taking care of others at the expense of their own well-being.

4. **Emotional Neglect:** Narcissistic parents often prioritize their own needs and emotions, leaving their children feeling neglected and emotionally unsupported. This can lead to a sense of emptiness and emotional detachment.

5. **Anxiety and Depression:** The inconsistent and unstable environment of a narcissistic family can contribute to the development of anxiety and depression. The constant need to navigate the unpredictable emotions of the narcissistic family member can be emotionally exhausting.

6. **Perfectionism:** Children in narcissistic families might feel pressured to achieve high standards to gain approval. This can lead to perfectionism and a fear of failure.

7. **Fear of Rejection:** Children in these families learn that their worth is contingent on meeting the expectations of the narcissistic family member. This can create a fear of rejection and abandonment if they don't meet these expectations.

8. **Difficulty Expressing Emotions:** In narcissistic families, emotions are often suppressed or invalidated. As a result, individuals might struggle to express their emotions and connect with their feelings, leading to difficulties in forming healthy emotional relationships.

9. **Trouble with Intimacy:** The lack of emotional connection and authenticity in narcissistic families can make it challenging for individuals to form intimate and trusting relationships in adulthood.

10. **Guilt and Shame:** Manipulation and blame are common in narcissistic family dynamics. Children might be made to feel guilty for asserting themselves or expressing their needs, leading to a pervasive sense of shame.

11. **Identity Issues:** Growing up in an environment where one's sense of self is undermined can lead to confusion about one's identity and values.

12. **Struggle with Trust:** Experiencing manipulation and emotional volatility within the family can make it difficult for individuals to trust others.

13. **Isolation:** Narcissistic families often discourage connections outside the family. This can result in social isolation and limited external support.

It's important to recognize that while these effects are common, everyone's experience is unique. Healing from the effects of growing up in a narcissistic family may involve therapy, support groups, self-discovery, and learning healthy coping mechanisms. With the right resources and strategies, individuals can work to overcome these challenges and build healthier relationships and a stronger sense of self.

Throughout this eBook, we will delve into the various aspects of healing from narcissistic family dynamics. We'll explore practical strategies, real-life anecdotes, and exercises designed to empower individuals to overcome the challenges they face and reclaim their sense of self-worth. By understanding the nuances of these dynamics and learning how to navigate them, you can embark on a journey towards healing, growth, and the creation of healthier relationships.

Breaking the Cycle: Understanding these roles and the power structure is crucial for breaking free from the cycle of dysfunction. Recognizing the impact of the narcissistic figure's dominance and identifying your role within the family dynamic opens the door to healing, self-empowerment, and the opportunity to reshape your relationships and life trajectory. By acknowledging these dynamics, you embark on a journey toward reclaiming your voice, setting boundaries, and nurturing a stronger sense of self.

Chapter 1

Recognizing Narcissistic Family Patterns

Growing up in a family where things aren't quite right can be confusing. This chapter will help you understand some of the signs that might show up in families where one person acts like they're the most important.

Identifying Narcissistic Behaviour

Have you ever met someone who always talks about themselves and wants everyone to think they're amazing? Well, in families, there could be a person like that too. They might be a parent or a big brother or sister. They always want to be the star of the show and expect everyone to pay attention to them. They might not care much about how others feel. This is what we call "narcissistic behaviour."

Common Roles and Dynamics

Narcissistic family units typically exhibit distinct roles that family members take on in response to the dominant and self-centred behaviour of the narcissistic parent or parents. It's important to note that these roles can vary in their intensity and presence depending on the specific dynamics of each family. Here are some common roles within narcissistic family units:

1. **Narcissistic Parent(s):** The central figure in the family, usually one or both parents, who display narcissistic traits or a full-blown narcissistic personality disorder. They often seek admiration, exploit others for their own gain, lack empathy, and

view themselves as superior. They dominate the family dynamic and prioritize their own needs over those of their children.

2. **Golden Child:** The child who is chosen by the narcissistic parent as the favoured one. The golden child receives preferential treatment, praise, and attention. They might be groomed to mirror the narcissistic parent's attitudes and behaviours. This child is often used to maintain the narcissistic parent's self-image.

3. **Scapegoat:** The scapegoat is the child who becomes the target of blame and criticism for the family's problems. They are often used as a way for the narcissistic parent to deflect attention from their own shortcomings. Scapegoats may also be more independent or defiant, which clashes with the family's need for control.

4. **Lost Child:** This child becomes emotionally withdrawn and avoids confrontation within the family. They often seek solace in solitude and might have a rich inner world. The lost child role is a coping mechanism to avoid the drama and chaos caused by the narcissistic parent. They may struggle with forming close relationships outside the family.

5. **Mascot/Clown:** The mascot or clown uses humour and distraction to defuse tension and keep the focus away from the family's dysfunctional dynamics. This role can be a way to cope with the stress and instability caused by the narcissistic parent.

6. **Caretaker/Enabler:** This role is often taken on by a child or spouse who assists the narcissistic parent in

maintaining their self-image and catering to their needs. They may enable the narcissistic behaviour by downplaying its impact, covering up for the parent's actions, or making excuses for their behaviour.

7. **Hero/Achiever:** The hero or achiever takes on the role of overachieving to compensate for the family's dysfunction. They strive to make the family look good on the outside, often excelling in academics, sports, or other areas. This role might be a way to seek approval and validation, especially from the narcissistic parent.

8. **Identified Patient:** This role involves a family member who exhibits emotional or behavioural issues that divert attention from the narcissistic parent's behaviour. The identified patient's struggles are highlighted, allowing the narcissistic parent to avoid addressing their own shortcomings.

It's important to remember that these roles can be fluid, and a single family member might adopt multiple roles at different times. Furthermore, not all narcissistic family units will have all these roles, and the dynamics can vary widely based on individual personalities and circumstances. Therapy and support are often crucial for individuals who have grown up within narcissistic family systems to heal and establish healthier relationships.

Example

Sarah grew up feeling like she was walking on eggshells around her father. No matter how hard she tried, he was never satisfied.

Explanation: Narcissistic family patterns often involve a dominant figure who seeks admiration and control, leaving other family members feeling invalidated and unseen.

Practical Exercise: Reflect on your family interactions. Do you notice patterns where one member consistently seeks attention or dismisses others' feelings?

Actionable Advice: Start observing and journaling about interactions. Understanding these patterns is the first step towards addressing them.

When the narcissistic individual is an older sibling rather than a parent, the dynamics within the family can still exhibit similar role patterns, although they might be somewhat different due to the hierarchical structure of sibling relationships. Here's how the roles might manifest in a family with a narcissistic older sibling:

1. **Narcissistic Sibling:** The older narcissistic sibling assumes a dominant role within the family. They may seek attention, admiration, and control over their younger siblings. They might display a sense of entitlement and lack of empathy, using their position to manipulate and exploit others for their own gain.

2. **Golden Sibling:** Like the golden child role, the golden sibling is the favoured one of the narcissistic older siblings. They might receive special treatment, praise, and privileges. The golden sibling might align with the narcissistic sibling's behaviours and attitudes to gain approval and avoid conflict.

3. **Scapegoat Sibling:** This role corresponds to the scapegoat in a narcissistic family unit led by a parent. The scapegoat sibling becomes the target of blame

and criticism, often being singled out for perceived shortcomings or issues within the family. They might bear the brunt of the narcissistic sibling's frustrations and manipulation.

4. **Lost Sibling:** Like the lost child role, the lost sibling becomes emotionally withdrawn and avoids confrontation with the narcissistic older sibling. They might seek refuge in solitude and develop coping mechanisms to deal with the emotional turmoil caused by the family dynamics.

5. **Mascot/Clown Sibling:** This sibling uses humour and diversion to ease tension and avoid confrontations with the narcissistic older sibling. They might act as a buffer to deflect attention from the family's dysfunction and keep the peace.

6. **Caretaker/Enabler Sibling:** This role might involve a sibling who caters to the needs of the narcissistic older sibling, much like the caretaker/enabler role in a parent-led narcissistic family. They might enable the narcissistic behaviour by downplaying its impact or making excuses for the older sibling's actions.

7. **Hero/Achiever Sibling:** Like the hero role, this sibling might overachieve to compensate for the family's dysfunction and the negative attention drawn by the narcissistic older sibling. They might excel in various areas to seek approval and validation.

8. **Identified Patient Sibling:** This role involves a sibling who displays emotional or behavioural issues that divert attention away from the narcissistic older sibling's behaviour. The identified patient sibling's struggles might be highlighted, allowing the

narcissistic sibling to avoid addressing their own actions.

It's important to recognize that the specific roles and dynamics within a family with a narcissistic older sibling can vary widely based on the personalities and interactions of the individuals involved. In these situations, seeking therapy and support can also be beneficial in helping family members understand and navigate the complexities of their relationships.

Chapter 2

Effects of Growing Up in a Narcissistic Family

Growing up in a family where one person's needs consistently overshadow others can leave deep emotional marks. Let's explore some of the common effects that might stick with you even as you grow older.

Low Self-Esteem and Insecurity

Imagine feeling like you're not good enough unless you're making the star person happy. Growing up with this constant need for approval can make you doubt your own worth. You might feel insecure about your abilities and always seek validation from others. This can affect your confidence and how you view yourself in various aspects of life.

Difficulty Setting Boundaries

In families with narcissistic dynamics, boundaries can become blurry. You might struggle to define what's okay and what's not. This makes it hard to say no or stand up for yourself, even when you should. You might end up sacrificing your own needs to avoid conflict or keep the peace, which can lead to further frustration and resentment.

Coping Mechanisms and Their Consequences

When dealing with a family where one person's needs are constantly prioritized, you develop ways to cope. These coping mechanisms can range from avoiding conflict to people-pleasing or even isolating yourself. While these tactics might have helped you survive the family environment, they can have consequences in your adult life.

For example, if you always put others' needs first to avoid conflict, you might find it hard to express your own needs and desires later on. If you're used to seeking validation from external sources, you might struggle with self-acceptance and self-love. Over time, these coping mechanisms can hinder your personal growth and overall well-being.

Understanding these effects is the first step toward healing. In the chapters to come, we'll discuss practical ways to address these challenges and start building a healthier sense of self and more balanced relationships.

Example.

Mark struggled with low self-esteem well into adulthood due to his mother's constant criticism.

Explanation: Growing up in a narcissistic family can lead to long-lasting effects like low self-esteem, anxiety, and difficulty forming healthy relationships.

Practical Exercise: List the effects you've noticed in your life due to your family dynamics. Acknowledge them without judgment.

Actionable Advice:

1. **Cultivate Self-Compassion:** Treat yourself with the kindness and understanding you deserved growing up. When you notice self-critical thoughts, replace them with affirming statements like "I am enough" or "I deserve love and respect."

2. **Positive Self-Talk:** Challenge negative beliefs about yourself by consciously replacing them with positive affirmations. Practice this daily, and gradually, you'll start believing these affirmations.

3. **Journaling for Healing:** Use journaling as a tool to explore your feelings, experiences, and thoughts. Write about the challenges you've faced and how they've affected you. This process can provide insights and promote emotional release.

Chapter 3

Healing the Self

Healing the self is a journey of personal growth and self-discovery aimed at recovering from emotional wounds, finding inner peace, and embracing your true essence. It involves acknowledging past pain, understanding its impact on your thoughts and behaviours, and actively working to release its hold on you.

Example

Emily's journey towards healing began when she started journaling about her experiences and how they made her feel.

Explanation: Healing starts with self-awareness. Acknowledge your emotions and experiences without self-blame.

Practical Exercise: Set aside time each day to reflect on your emotions. Write down your thoughts without censoring yourself.

Actionable Advice: Allow yourself to feel and validate your emotions. This is a crucial step towards healing.

Healing the self is about cultivating self-awareness, self-compassion, and self-love.

1. **Cultivating Self-Awareness:** Self-awareness involves paying close attention to your thoughts, emotions, and behaviours. It's about understanding why you react in certain ways and recognizing patterns in your thoughts

and actions. By becoming more self-aware, you can gain insights into your strengths, weaknesses, and triggers, allowing you to make conscious choices and better understand the impact of your experiences on your current self.

2. **Self-Compassion:** Self-compassion is the practice of treating yourself with the same kindness and understanding that you would offer to a friend. It's about acknowledging your imperfections and mistakes without harsh self-judgment. Self-compassion involves being gentle with yourself during challenging times and offering support and encouragement rather than criticism. It's a way to foster a positive and nurturing relationship with yourself.

3. **Self-Love:** Self-love is the deep appreciation and care you have for your own well-being and happiness. It's recognizing your inherent worth and valuing yourself for who you are, regardless of external achievements or validations. Self-love involves prioritizing your needs, setting boundaries, and making choices that honour your physical, emotional, and mental health. It's about recognizing that you deserve happiness, fulfilment, and a life that aligns with your values and aspirations.

Healing the self is a process of letting go of limiting beliefs, negative patterns, and self-doubt.

1. **Letting Go of Limiting Beliefs:** Limiting beliefs are thoughts that hold you back from reaching your full potential. Letting go of these beliefs involves recognizing and challenging the negative thoughts that undermine your confidence and aspirations. It's about

replacing them with positive, empowering beliefs that support your growth and progress.

2. **Breaking Negative Patterns:** Negative patterns are repetitive behaviours or reactions that keep you stuck in unproductive cycles. Breaking these patterns requires identifying triggers and recognizing how they contribute to your challenges. It involves consciously choosing alternative actions and responses that align with your goals and values, ultimately creating healthier behaviours.

3. **Overcoming Self-Doubt:** Self-doubt is the uncertainty and lack of confidence in your abilities. Overcoming self-doubt involves acknowledging your fears and insecurities while reframing them as opportunities for growth. It's about recognizing your achievements and focusing on your strengths, gradually building a sense of self-assurance that counters self-doubt's hold on you.

You will want to replace them with positive affirmations, healthy coping mechanisms, and a renewed sense of purpose.

1. **Positive Affirmations:** Positive affirmations are short, uplifting statements you repeat to yourself to challenge and replace negative thoughts. They help reshape your mindset by focusing on your strengths and potential. By regularly using positive affirmations, you can boost your self-esteem, cultivate a positive outlook, and gradually shift your internal dialogue.

2. **Healthy Coping Mechanisms:** Healthy coping mechanisms are constructive ways to manage stress,

emotions, and challenges. They involve strategies that don't harm your well-being or rely on avoidance. Examples include practicing mindfulness, engaging in physical activity, seeking support from friends, engaging in creative outlets, and learning relaxation techniques. These mechanisms help you navigate difficulties in a way that promotes emotional well-being.

3. **Renewed Sense of Purpose:** A renewed sense of purpose involves reconnecting with what gives your life meaning and direction. It's about identifying your passions, values, and goals, and aligning your actions with them. When you have a clear sense of purpose, you're more motivated, resilient, and focused on creating a fulfilling life that reflects who you truly are.

Through this process, you can rebuild your self-esteem, reconnect with your authentic identity, and create a life that aligns with your values and aspirations.

Growing up in a narcissistic family can leave you feeling lost and disconnected from who you truly are. But there's hope for healing and rediscovery.

This chapter will guide you on a journey to nurture your inner self and embrace your worth.

Cultivating Self-Awareness

Nurturing self-awareness is the first step toward healing. Take time to explore your feelings, reactions, and patterns that have been shaped by your family dynamics. Here's how:

- **Daily Reflection:** Dedicate a few minutes each day to reflect on your emotions and experiences. What triggered you today? How did you respond? This practice helps you become more conscious of your internal world.

- **Journal Your Journey:** Write down your thoughts, dreams, and challenges. Journaling provides a safe space to express yourself and discover patterns that might be holding you back.

- **Mindful Moments:** Practice mindfulness by tuning into your senses during daily activities. Engaging fully in the present moment can help you break free from past patterns.

Rebuilding Self-Esteem

Self-esteem refers to how you see and value yourself. It's the opinion and feelings you have about your own abilities, qualities, and worth as a person. Having healthy self-esteem means having a positive and realistic view of yourself, feeling confident in your abilities, and recognizing your value even in the face of challenges or mistakes. It's about treating yourself with kindness, respect, and understanding, and believing that you deserve happiness and success. Healthy self-esteem is essential for overall well-being and a positive outlook on life.

Years of being belittled or overshadowed can take a toll on your self-esteem. Rebuilding it requires patience and self-compassion. Try these practical strategies:

- **Celebrate Small Wins:** Acknowledge your achievements, no matter how small they might seem. Each step forward is a victory that deserves recognition.

- **Positive Affirmations:** Create a list of positive affirmations that challenge negative beliefs. Repeat these affirmations daily to gradually shift your self-perception.
- **Challenge Inner Critic:** Pay attention to your inner critic and question its validity. Would you say these things to a friend? Treat yourself with the same kindness you'd show to others.

Reclaiming Your Identity

Growing up, your identity might have been overshadowed by family roles. Now, it's time to reclaim who you are.

Reconnecting with your authentic self refers to the process of rediscovering and embracing your identity, free from external influences, expectations, and roles that you might have adopted due to family dynamics or societal pressures. It involves peeling away the layers of conditioning, fears, and insecurities that have accumulated over time and getting in touch with your genuine desires, values, interests, and passions.

When you reconnect with your authentic self, you align your choices, actions, and life path with what resonates deeply within you. It's about living in alignment with your true nature, listening to your intuition, and making decisions that honour who you are at your core. This process often involves letting go of what no longer serves you, shedding the masks you might have worn, and embracing your uniqueness without fear of judgment.

In essence, reconnecting with your authentic self is a transformative journey of self-discovery that leads to greater self-acceptance, inner peace, and a life that feels genuinely fulfilling and meaningful to you.

Here's how to reconnect with your authentic self:

- **Explore Your Passions:** Engage in activities you genuinely enjoy, even if they were discouraged in your family. Rediscover hobbies that resonate with your true interests.

- **Set Personal Goals:** Identify goals that are aligned with your values and aspirations. Pursue these goals as a way of honouring your individual journey.

- **Surround Yourself with Positivity:** Choose to spend time with people who uplift and support you. Surrounding yourself with positivity can reinforce your sense of self-worth.

- **Self-Expression:** Find ways to express yourself authentically. This could be through art, writing, music, or any creative outlet that resonates with you.

Remember, healing takes time, and the journey is unique for everyone. Be patient with yourself and embrace the progress you make. Reclaiming your sense of self is a transformative process that will empower you to live a more authentic and fulfilling life.

Chapter 4

Setting Healthy Boundaries

Example

Alex had to learn that saying "no" was not selfish, but an act of self-care.

Explanation: Narcissistic dynamics often involve disregarding boundaries. Setting and maintaining boundaries is essential for your well-being.

Practical Exercise: Identify a situation where you need to establish a boundary. Practice assertive communication to express your needs.

Actionable Advice: Start small and gradually enforce boundaries. Over time, you'll feel more empowered.

Growing up in a narcissistic family often means that personal boundaries were either ignored or violated. This chapter will empower you to establish and maintain healthy boundaries that respect your needs and well-being.

Personal boundaries refer to the emotional, physical, and psychological limits that you establish to protect your well-being, values, and sense of self-respect. These boundaries help define what is acceptable and unacceptable behaviour in your interactions with others. They ensure that your needs, feelings, and values are honoured and that you maintain a healthy level of self-care and self-respect.

Personal boundaries can vary from person to person and situation to situation.

They encompass various aspects:

1. **Emotional Boundaries:** These boundaries define how much you share about your thoughts, feelings, and experiences with others. They prevent emotional manipulation, invasion of your privacy, and the feeling of being overwhelmed by others' emotions.

2. **Physical Boundaries:** Physical boundaries involve your personal space, touch, and physical interactions. They help you feel safe and respected, preventing others from invading your personal space without your consent.

3. **Mental Boundaries:** Mental boundaries involve protecting your thoughts, beliefs, and opinions. They ensure that you can form your own judgments and decisions without being influenced or manipulated by others.

Establishing and maintaining personal boundaries is essential for healthy relationships, self-respect, and maintaining your emotional well-being. They allow you to communicate your needs, protect your energy, and create a balanced and respectful environment for yourself and those around you.

Understanding Personal Boundaries

Personal boundaries are like your own invisible lines that define your emotional, physical, and psychological limits. They help protect your self-esteem, values, and overall sense of safety. Here's how to understand them:

- **Types of Boundaries:** Emotional boundaries involve safeguarding your feelings, physical boundaries involve personal space and touch, and mental boundaries involve maintaining your own thoughts and opinions.

- **Signs of Weak Boundaries:** You might feel overwhelmed by others' demands, struggle to say no, or find yourself constantly sacrificing your needs to please others.

Strategies for Implementing Boundaries

Setting and enforcing boundaries can be empowering, but it requires practice. Here are strategies to help you implement healthy boundaries effectively:

- **Identify Your Limits:** Reflect on what you're comfortable with and what makes you feel uncomfortable. Know your limits in various aspects of your life.

- **Communicate Clearly:** Express your boundaries calmly and assertively. Use "I" statements to communicate how certain actions or behaviours affect you.

- **Practice Self-Care:** Prioritize your own well-being without feeling guilty. Make self-care a non-negotiable part of your routine.

- **Start Small:** Begin by setting boundaries in less challenging situations. As you build confidence, you can address more complex issues.

Navigating Pushback and Resistance

As you establish boundaries, you might encounter resistance, especially from those accustomed to the old dynamics. Here's how to handle pushback:

- **Stay Firm:** Stick to your boundaries even if others protest. Remind yourself that your well-being matters.

- **Use Support Systems:** Seek support from friends, therapists, or support groups. Surround yourself with people who understand and respect your journey.

- **Set Consequences:** Establish consequences for those who consistently disregard your boundaries. Consistent enforcement helps establish your commitment.

- **Self-Affirmation:** Remind yourself why setting boundaries is important for your growth and well-being. Positive self-talk can counter doubts and fears.

Remember: Setting boundaries is an act of self-love and respect. It's about valuing your needs as much as you value others'. While it might be challenging at first, it's a crucial step toward reclaiming your autonomy and creating healthier relationships.

Chapter 5

Communication and Relationships

Example.

Lisa improved her relationship with her sister by using "I" statements and active listening.

Explanation: Healthy communication is key. Use "I" statements to express how you feel and practice active listening to foster understanding.

Practical Exercise: Choose a family member to have an open conversation with. Use "I" statements to express your feelings.

Actionable Advice: Practice empathetic listening. This creates a safe space for open communication.

Navigating healthy communication and forming positive relationships can be especially challenging after growing up in a narcissistic family. This chapter will guide you in developing effective communication skills and fostering supportive connections.

Healthy communication is the effective exchange of thoughts, feelings, and information between individuals in a respectful and supportive manner. It involves both verbal and nonverbal communication that promotes understanding, trust, and connection while minimizing misunderstandings and conflicts.

Key aspects of healthy communication include:

1. **Active Listening:** Giving full attention to the speaker without interrupting or preparing your response. It shows respect and helps you truly understand the message being conveyed.

2. **Empathy:** Understanding and acknowledging the emotions and perspective of the other person. It creates a sense of emotional connection and validation.

3. **Clarity and Transparency:** Expressing thoughts and feelings clearly and honestly. Avoiding vague or ambiguous language prevents confusion.

4. **Respectful Tone:** Using a tone of voice and body language that conveys respect and openness. Avoiding aggressive or defensive tones helps maintain a positive atmosphere.

5. **Feedback:** Providing constructive feedback that focuses on behaviour rather than making personal attacks. This promotes growth and improvement.

6. **Nonverbal Communication:** Being aware of body language, facial expressions, and gestures, which often convey feelings that words might not express.

7. **Conflict Resolution:** Addressing disagreements in a calm and collaborative manner. Listening actively and seeking compromise or solutions that benefit both parties.

8. **Boundaries:** Recognizing and respecting personal boundaries in communication. Avoiding intrusive questions or topics that might make someone uncomfortable.

Healthy communication contributes to building strong relationships, resolving conflicts, and fostering mutual understanding. It encourages open dialogue, ensures that everyone's voice is heard, and creates an environment of trust and emotional safety.

Learning Healthy Communication

Healthy communication forms the foundation of strong and harmonious relationships. It's a skill that can be developed over time and holds the power to enhance understanding, minimize conflicts, and build trust. Here's a closer look at how to cultivate healthy communication:

Active Listening: Active listening is a vital aspect of healthy communication. It goes beyond simply hearing words; it involves giving your full attention to the speaker, both verbally and nonverbally. When you actively listen:

- **Maintain Eye Contact:** By making eye contact, you show that you are fully engaged and genuinely interested in what the speaker is saying.

- **Avoid Interrupting:** Let the speaker finish their thoughts before responding. Interrupting can disrupt the flow of their message and convey impatience.

- **Provide Nonverbal Feedback:** Nodding, smiling, and using facial expressions demonstrate that you are actively following the conversation.

- **Ask Clarifying Questions:** If something is unclear, ask questions to ensure you grasp the speaker's intended message.

- **Avoid Distractions:** Put away distractions like phones or other devices. Being present in the moment shows respect for the speaker.

Open-Mindedness: Healthy communication thrives when you approach conversations with an open mind. This means:

- **Suspending Judgment:** Avoid making immediate judgments or assumptions. Instead, allow the speaker to express themselves fully before forming an opinion.

- **Exploring Different Perspectives:** Be willing to consider viewpoints that differ from your own. This encourages a respectful exchange of ideas.

- **Cultivating Empathy:** Put yourself in the speaker's shoes to understand their feelings and experiences. Empathy fosters connection and validates their emotions.

Honesty and Transparency: Being honest and transparent in your communication builds trust and authenticity. When practicing honesty:

- **Express Your Thoughts and Feelings:** Share your own perspective openly and truthfully. This creates an environment where others feel comfortable doing the same.

- **Avoid Deception:** Steer clear of exaggerations, lies, or half-truths. Honesty paves the way for genuine interactions.

- **Address Challenges Directly:** Tackle difficult conversations head-on. Openly discussing issues helps prevent misunderstandings and promotes resolution.

- **Accept Vulnerability:** Sharing your genuine thoughts and feelings, even if they make you vulnerable, encourages deeper connections.

By integrating these principles of healthy communication into your interactions, you create an environment where people feel heard, respected, and valued. Remember that mastering these skills takes practice, but the rewards in terms of improved relationships and mutual understanding are well worth the effort.

Strategies for Assertive Communication

Assertive communication is a powerful tool that allows you to express your thoughts, feelings, and needs in a direct and respectful manner. By practicing assertive communication, you can create open and honest interactions while maintaining a sense of self-respect and consideration for others. Here are strategies to help you communicate assertively:

- **Use "I" Statements:** "I" statements are a constructive way to express your feelings and needs without blaming or accusing others. By using "I" statements, you take ownership of your emotions and encourage a non-confrontational dialogue. For instance:
- **Instead of saying,** "You never listen to me," try "I feel unheard when our conversations get interrupted."
- **Set Boundaries:** Clear communication of your boundaries is essential for maintaining your well-being and respecting your personal limits. When setting boundaries:
- **Be Explicit:** Clearly state what behaviour is acceptable and what is not. For example, "I appreciate your company, but I'm uncomfortable when personal topics are discussed."
- **Practice Calmness:** Staying composed during conversations ensures that your message is heard and understood without escalating conflicts. When practicing calmness:
- **Control Your Emotions:** Take deep breaths and maintain control over your emotional reactions. This prevents misunderstandings that can arise from reacting impulsively.
- **Choose the Right Time:** Address sensitive topics when you and the other person are calm and receptive. Timing plays a significant role in effective communication.
- **Respond, Don't React:** Instead of reacting impulsively, respond thoughtfully to what's being said.

This demonstrates assertiveness and a measured approach.

- **Use Empathy:** Show empathy toward the other person's perspective, even if you disagree. This can help keep the conversation respectful and constructive.

By integrating these assertive communication strategies into your interactions, you can express your thoughts and feelings confidently while maintaining respect for both you and others. As you practice, you'll find that assertive communication empowers you to navigate conversations with self-assurance and create a healthier and more open communication style.

Nurturing Supportive Relationships

Creating and nurturing supportive relationships beyond your family circle is essential for your emotional well-being and personal growth. These relationships provide a positive and nurturing environment where you can thrive. Here's how to foster such connections:

Choose Wisely: Surround yourself with people who genuinely uplift, respect, and appreciate you for who you are. Choosing friends and companions who align with your values and support your well-being contributes to a healthier social circle.

Distance from Negativity: Recognize relationships that drain your energy or bring negativity into your life. Create distance from individuals who perpetuate toxic dynamics.

Reciprocity: Healthy relationships are built on a foundation of mutual care and effort. Focus on connections where both parties contribute and support each other.

Give and Take: Strive for a balanced exchange of support, where both parties benefit from the relationship. This reciprocity creates a sense of trust and reliability.

Open Communication: True friends and allies are willing to listen and understand your experiences. Foster open communication by discussing your past experiences and your journey to healing with trusted individuals.

Share Your Story: Opening about your past can lead to deeper connections and a sense of shared understanding. This vulnerability often leads to reciprocal sharing and emotional support.

Empathy: Seek out relationships with individuals who exhibit empathy and understanding. These qualities create an emotionally safe space where you can express your feelings and experiences without fear of judgment.

Empathetic Connections: Build connections with those who validate your emotions and demonstrate compassion. Such relationships offer a sense of belonging and emotional support.

Remember: Building and maintaining supportive relationships is an ongoing process. It requires continuous effort and attention to ensure that you're surrounded by people who uplift and contribute positively to your journey. By practicing healthy communication and choosing relationships that align with your well-being, you create a network of allies that enhance your overall happiness and personal development.

Chapter 6
Coping with Emotional Challenges

Example: Jack found solace in mindfulness practices that helped him manage anxiety triggered by family interactions.

Explanation: Narcissistic family dynamics can lead to emotional challenges. Mindfulness and self-care techniques are valuable tools.

Practical Exercise: Try a mindfulness meditation or deep-breathing exercise. Notice how it affects your emotional state.

Actionable Advice: Incorporate mindfulness into your daily routine. It can help you manage stress and regulate emotions.

Growing up in a narcissistic family can leave you facing various emotional challenges. This chapter is designed to equip you with strategies to manage anxiety, depression, and develop emotional resilience while prioritizing self-care.

Managing Anxiety and Depression

Growing up in a narcissistic family dynamic can leave a lasting impact on your emotional well-being, often leading to heightened anxiety and even depression. These emotional challenges can manifest due to the constant stress, uncertainty, and invalidation that are often present in such environments. Here's how you can effectively manage anxiety and depression stemming from these experiences:

Seek Professional Help:

- If anxiety or depression is significantly affecting your daily life, seeking the guidance of a mental health professional is crucial. Therapists or counsellors can provide you with tailored strategies to manage your symptoms and work through the underlying issues.

Practice Mindfulness: Mindfulness techniques offer valuable tools to manage anxiety and depression. Mindfulness involves being present in the moment, which can help you detach from anxious thoughts or depressive rumination. Techniques like deep breathing, meditation, and body scans can help you ground yourself and reduce the intensity of overwhelming emotions.

Challenge Negative Thoughts: Narcissistic family dynamics often contribute to negative self-perceptions and distorted thinking patterns. Learn to recognize these negative thoughts and question their validity. Replace them with more balanced and realistic thoughts that counter the self-criticism and self-doubt often associated with anxiety and depression.

Cultivate a Supportive Network:
Building a supportive network of friends, family, or even support groups can provide emotional validation and understanding. Sharing your experiences with others who empathize can alleviate feelings of isolation and offer a sense of belonging.

Engage in Self-Compassion:
Develop self-compassion by treating yourself with the same kindness and understanding you'd offer to a friend. Be patient with yourself as you navigate the challenges arising

from your family dynamics. Avoid self-blame and instead focus on your growth and healing journey.

Remember: Managing anxiety and depression requires a multi-faceted approach. While these strategies can provide valuable guidance, it's important to tailor your coping mechanisms to your unique needs. Be patient with yourself and celebrate each step you take toward improved emotional well-being. If your symptoms are severe or persistent, seeking professional help is essential to ensure you receive the support you need.

Developing Emotional Resilience

Emotional resilience is your ability to adapt, cope, and bounce back from challenging or distressing situations. It's the capacity to withstand and navigate life's ups and downs while maintaining a sense of emotional well-being. Emotional resilience doesn't mean avoiding difficulties; instead, it involves facing them head-on with a positive attitude, the ability to manage stress, and a belief in your own ability to overcome adversity.

Key aspects of emotional resilience include:

Adaptability: Resilient individuals are flexible and able to adjust their mindset and strategies in response to changing circumstances. They view challenges as opportunities for growth and learning.

Positive Outlook: Emotional resilience involves maintaining a relatively optimistic perspective, even during tough times. Resilient individuals find silver linings and focus on solutions rather than dwelling on problems.

Emotional Regulation: Resilience includes the ability to manage and regulate your emotions effectively. You're better equipped to handle stress, anxiety, and negative emotions without being overwhelmed by them.

Support System: Building and maintaining a strong network of social support contributes to emotional resilience. Having people to lean on during challenging times provides emotional validation and encouragement.

Problem-Solving Skills: Resilient individuals are proactive in addressing challenges. They break down problems into manageable steps and work toward finding solutions.

Self-Compassion: Being kind to yourself and practicing self-compassion are crucial elements of emotional resilience. Treating yourself with understanding and patience during difficult times helps you maintain a sense of self-worth.

Emotional resilience isn't a fixed trait; it's a skill that can be developed and strengthened over time. By cultivating these attributes and strategies, you can enhance your ability to navigate life's challenges with greater ease and maintain your emotional well-being.

Building emotional resilience equips you with the tools to handle life's challenges with strength and grace. Here's how you can foster emotional resilience:

Build a Support System: Create a network of individuals who uplift and understand you. Surround yourself with supportive friends, family members, or consider seeking guidance from a therapist. Having people who genuinely care and provide a listening ear during tough times can significantly bolster your emotional well-being.

Develop Problem-Solving Skills: Enhance your problem-solving abilities by breaking down challenges into smaller, manageable steps. Instead of feeling overwhelmed by the enormity of a problem, focus on practical solutions. This approach empowers you to act and make progress, which contributes to a sense of accomplishment and resilience.

Practice Adaptability: Embrace change as a natural part of life and view it as an opportunity for growth. Cultivating adaptability allows you to navigate uncertainties and unexpected situations with a more open mind. Embracing change fosters a positive attitude and reduces the fear associated with the unknown.

Remember, building emotional resilience is a journey that involves continuous practice and growth. By cultivating a strong support system, honing problem-solving skills, and embracing adaptability, you'll be better prepared to face life's challenges with confidence and a greater sense of inner strength.

Practicing Self-Care

Prioritizing self-care is a vital component of maintaining your emotional well-being and building resilience. Self-care involves consciously taking actions that nurture and rejuvenate your mind, body, and soul. Here's how you can integrate self-care into your routine:

Set Boundaries: Establishing clear boundaries is a form of self-care that safeguards your time, energy, and emotional space. Learn to say "no" when necessary and communicate your limits to others. Setting boundaries empowers you to create a balanced and healthy life.

Engage in Activities You Enjoy: Dedicating time to activities you genuinely enjoy is a powerful self-care practice. Engaging in hobbies, pursuits, and experiences that bring you joy, relaxation, and a sense of accomplishment boosts your mood and overall well-being.

Prioritize Physical Health: Physical health and emotional well-being are closely connected. Regular exercise, balanced nutrition, and sufficient sleep contribute to stable moods and increased resilience. Engaging in physical activities that you enjoy not only benefits your body but also uplifts your spirits.

Seek Pleasure: Engaging in activities that bring you pleasure is a vital aspect of self-care. Whether it's reading a book, spending time in nature, exploring your creativity, or enjoying a hobby, these activities provide a sense of fulfilment and relaxation.

Practice Mindfulness: Mindfulness, or being present in the moment, is a self-care practice that helps you connect with your thoughts, feelings, and surroundings. Mindful activities such as meditation, deep breathing, or simply taking a quiet walk can help reduce stress and promote emotional well-being.

Remember that self-care is not a luxury; it's a necessary practice that supports your emotional resilience. By setting boundaries, engaging in activities that bring you joy, prioritizing your physical health, and seeking out pleasurable experiences, you create a foundation of self-love and nourishment that strengthens your ability to face life's challenges with grace and strength.

Chapter 7

Strategies for Healing

Navigating the journey of healing from the effects of a narcissistic family dynamic requires intentional and effective strategies.

"Strategies for Healing" are the various approaches, techniques, and practices that you can use to address emotional wounds, overcome challenges, and work towards overall well-being and personal growth. These strategies are designed to support you in your journey of healing from difficult experiences, such as those stemming from a narcissistic family dynamic.

In this chapter, we'll explore key approaches to support your healing process and empower you to reclaim your well-being.

1. Seeking Professional Help:

Professional guidance plays a pivotal role in your healing journey. Therapists, counsellors, or psychologists possess the expertise to help you address underlying emotional wounds, develop coping strategies, and guide you toward lasting transformation. They offer a safe space to explore your experiences and provide tailored techniques to promote healing.

2. Therapeutic Relationships: The Power of Healing Bonds

Building a strong therapeutic relationship is a cornerstone of effective healing and personal growth. This connection between you and your therapist provides a safe and non-judgmental space where you can explore your thoughts, emotions, and concerns. This relationship is grounded in trust, understanding, and empathy, and it plays a pivotal role in your journey towards emotional well-being. Here's how it works:

Expressing Without Judgment: In a therapeutic relationship, you're free to express your thoughts and emotions without fear of criticism or judgment. This environment of acceptance and validation encourages you to be open about your experiences, even those that might be difficult or painful.

Unbiased Perspectives: Therapists bring an external and unbiased perspective to your experiences. They can help you view situations from different angles and challenge negative thought patterns. This fresh perspective often reveals insights that might have been overlooked.

Tools and Coping Strategies: Therapists offer a toolkit of coping strategies, techniques, and skills tailored to your unique needs. These tools empower you **to** manage challenges, regulate emotions, and navigate difficult situations more effectively.

Guidance and Insights: Through open conversations and guided exploration, therapists provide insights into your behaviour, patterns, and motivations. This self-awareness is crucial for identifying areas of growth and working towards meaningful change.

Validation and Empathy: Experiencing validation and empathy from a trained professional can be immensely healing. It reinforces that your experiences and emotions are valid, helping you build self-esteem and self-compassion.

Collaborative Approach: Therapeutic relationships are collaborative partnerships. You and your therapist work together to set goals, track progress, and make decisions about the direction of your healing journey.

Safe Space for Growth: A therapeutic relationship creates a safe space where you can challenge yourself, explore uncomfortable topics, and experiment with new ways of thinking and behaving. This environment of trust nurtures your personal growth and resilience.

Remember that building a therapeutic relationship takes time, and finding the right therapist is essential. When you establish a strong therapeutic alliance, you create a foundation for healing, self-discovery, and lasting positive change in your life.

3. Mindfulness and Meditation:

Mindfulness and meditation are transformative practices that cultivate self-awareness, reduce stress, and promote emotional balance. Incorporating mindfulness into your daily routine encourages you to stay present, observe your thoughts without judgment, and nurture a sense of inner peace.

- **Practice Presence:** Mindfulness involves focusing on the present moment, acknowledging your thoughts and emotions without attachment. This practice can alleviate rumination and anxiety.

- **Meditation:** Regular meditation sessions offer a dedicated time to quiet the mind, enhance self-reflection, and encourage a positive outlook. Meditation can help you develop emotional regulation skills.

4. Cathartic Release through Creative Expression:

Engaging in creative activities provides a unique and powerful outlet for processing complex emotions in a constructive and therapeutic way. Here's how creative expression can serve as a cathartic release:

Channelling Emotions: Creative activities such as painting, writing, or playing a musical instrument enable you to channel intense emotions into the process. By externalizing your feelings through creative outlets, you give shape and form to emotions that might be difficult to express verbally.

Non-Verbal Expression: Emotions can sometimes surpass the limitations of language. Creative expression offers a means to communicate emotions without relying solely on words. This can be particularly beneficial when feelings are overwhelming or difficult to articulate.

Release of Tension: The act of creating allows you to release pent-up tension, stress, and emotional energy. As you immerse yourself in the creative process, you may feel a sense of relief and lightness as negative emotions find an outlet.

Empowerment and Control: Engaging in creative endeavours empowers you to take control over your emotional experiences. You can transform challenging emotions into something tangible and beautiful, shifting your perspective from feeling controlled by your emotions to harnessing them for growth.

Healing through Creation: The act of creating itself can be inherently healing. The focused engagement required by creative activities often brings a sense of mindfulness and presence, allowing you to temporarily step away from distressing thoughts and emotions.

Self-Discovery: Through creative expression, you might uncover insights about your emotions, triggers, and inner world. The process of creation can lead to greater self-awareness and a deeper understanding of your experiences.

Remember that creative expression doesn't require artistic expertise; it's about the process and the emotions it evokes. Whether it's painting, writing, dancing, or any other creative outlet, allowing yourself to explore and express your emotions through these activities can contribute to your overall healing and emotional well-being.

Chapter 8

Practical Steps for Building a Stronger Self

In this chapter, we delve into actionable steps that empower you to build a stronger sense of self, cultivate positive beliefs, and create daily routines that support your well-being. These practical strategies are designed to facilitate personal growth and enhance your overall quality of life.

Affirmations for Positive Self-Beliefs:

Affirmations are powerful statements that help reshape your self-perception and foster a positive mindset. By repeating affirmations regularly, you can gradually replace self-doubt with self-empowerment. Here's how they work:

- **Creating Affirmations:** Develop affirmations that counter negative self-talk and focus on your strengths, resilience, and potential. For example, "I am worthy of love and respect."

- **Daily Practice:** Integrate affirmations into your daily routine. Repeat them in the morning or whenever you need a boost of positivity. Over time, they can help rewire your thought patterns.

- **Belief Reinforcement:** Affirmations help reinforce positive self-beliefs. By consistently affirming your worth and capabilities, you gradually build a stronger foundation of self-confidence.

Positive affirmations can be a powerful tool to help shift negative thought patterns, build self-esteem, and cultivate a more positive self-image. Here are some affirmations that individuals who have grown up in narcissistic family dynamics might find helpful. Remember to choose the affirmations that resonate with you the most:

I am worthy of love and respect, just as I am.

I deserve to set and maintain healthy boundaries in all areas of my life.

I am not defined by my past; I have the power to create my own future.

I am enough. I don't need to seek validation from others to feel whole.

I release the need to control things outside of my control.

I am capable of making my own decisions and choices.

I am free to express my thoughts and feelings without fear of judgment.

I deserve happiness, and I am allowed to prioritize my own well-being.

I am resilient, and I can overcome any challenges that come my way.

I am worthy of healthy and loving relationships that support my growth.

I trust my intuition and believe in my own inner wisdom.

I release any guilt or shame that does not belong to me.

I am proud of my progress and the person I am becoming.

I am not responsible for the emotions or actions of others.

I embrace change as an opportunity for growth and transformation.

I am not defined by the expectations of others; I define my own worth.

I am deserving of self-care and the time I invest in myself.

I am worthy of forgiveness, especially from myself.

I am strong and capable of facing challenges with courage and grace.

I am loved and valued by those who see and appreciate the real me.

When using positive affirmations, remember to say them with conviction and repetition. It can be helpful to incorporate them into your daily routine, such as repeating them in the morning or before bedtime, writing them down in a journal, or creating visual reminders in your living space. Over time, these affirmations can help shift your mindset and promote positive self-beliefs.

Journaling Prompts for Self-Reflection: Unveiling Your Inner World

Journaling is a powerful tool that offers you a window into your inner thoughts, feelings, and experiences. It's a form of self-expression that enhances self-awareness and fosters personal growth. By capturing your thoughts on paper, you can gain insights, identify patterns, and promote emotional healing. Here's how you can harness the potential of journaling for self-reflection:

Set Aside Time: Designate a regular time for journaling in your day. Whether it's in the morning as you set intentions for the day or in the evening as you reflect on your experiences, consistency is key. This dedicated time creates a ritual of self-discovery.

Prompts for Exploration: Journaling prompts act as guideposts for your reflections. These prompts encourage you to explore various dimensions of your life, emotions, and experiences. For instance, prompts like "What are my proudest accomplishments?" prompt you to acknowledge your achievements and strengths. Other prompts might include "What challenges have I overcome?" or "What does happiness mean to me?" These prompts gently steer your thoughts in directions that promote self-discovery and insight.

Honesty and Openness: Approach your journaling practice with honesty and openness. Remember that your journal is a judgment-free space—it's your sanctuary to express your thoughts, feelings, and experiences authentically. Writing without filters allows you to confront difficult emotions, confront challenges, and celebrate your triumphs. This authenticity leads to deeper self-awareness and personal growth.

Healing Through Expression: Writing down your thoughts and feelings is cathartic. It provides a release valve for pent-up emotions and allows you to process experiences that might be difficult to discuss verbally. By acknowledging and expressing your feelings on paper, you create a pathway for emotional healing and growth.

Personal Insight and Growth: As you consistently journal, you'll notice patterns, trends, and shifts in your emotions and thoughts. This self-awareness can lead to personal insights that contribute to your growth and self-improvement journey.

Remember that journaling is a flexible practice—you can tailor it to suit your preferences and needs. Whether you're exploring your emotions, setting goals, or reflecting on challenges, the act of journaling serves as a mirror to your inner world, offering you a deeper understanding of yourself and promoting your overall well-being.

Implementing Healthy Daily Routines: Nurturing Your Well-Being

Healthy daily routines play a pivotal role in fostering emotional well-being and personal growth. By creating structure and stability, these routines contribute to a balanced and fulfilling life. Here's how you can implement healthy daily routines to enhance your overall well-being:

Prioritize Self-Care: Allocate time each day for self-care activities that nurture your physical, mental, and emotional health. Engage in exercises that you enjoy, practice meditation or mindfulness, or immerse yourself in hobbies that bring you joy. Self-care reinforces your self-worth and supports your well-being.

Establish Consistency: Consistency is the foundation of forming healthy habits. Set specific times for essential tasks, such as waking up, meals, and winding down before sleep. Establishing a consistent routine helps regulate your body's internal clock and promotes better sleep quality.

Include Mindful Moments: Incorporate moments of mindfulness throughout your day. Take breaks to practice deep breathing, engage in brief meditation sessions, or simply enjoy a few minutes of stillness. These mindful pauses help reduce stress, increase focus, and bring a sense of calm to your daily life.

Practice Gratitude: Allocate time to express gratitude for the positive aspects of your day. This practice can be as simple as jotting down a few things you're thankful for or reflecting on moments that brought you joy. Gratitude promotes a positive outlook, shifts your focus from challenges to blessings, and enhances your overall well-being.

Customize Your Routine: Tailor your daily routine to suit your preferences and needs. Recognize that everyone's ideal routine might differ based on personal commitments, work schedules, and lifestyle. Customization ensures that your routine is practical and sustainable.

Benefits of Healthy Routines: Implementing healthy daily routines offers several benefits for your well-being and personal growth:

- **Structure:** Routines provide structure, which can reduce feelings of chaos and enhance your overall sense of control.

- **Stability:** Regular routines create a sense of stability, which can be particularly comforting during times of change or uncertainty.

- **Mind-Body Connection:** Prioritizing self-care and mindfulness strengthens the connection between your mind and body, fostering holistic well-being.

- **Positive Outlook:** Engaging in gratitude and self-care practices can shift your perspective towards a more positive and optimistic outlook on life.

By incorporating self-care, consistency, mindfulness, and gratitude into your daily routine, you create a lifestyle that supports your well-being, personal growth, and overall quality of life. These practices, combined with affirmations and journaling, contribute to nurturing a stronger sense of self, fostering self-compassion, and embracing positive change.

Chapter 9

Case Studies and Real-Life Examples: Insights from Healing Journeys

In this chapter, we dive into the real-life experiences of individuals who have navigated the challenges of healing from narcissistic family dynamics. By examining their stories, you'll gain insights into practical applications of healing strategies and witness the transformational power of personal growth. Here's what you can expect:

Profiles of Individuals and Their Healing Journeys:

These profiles provide a glimpse into the lives of individuals who have embarked on journeys of healing. You'll learn about their backgrounds, struggles, and the pivotal moments that spurred their desire for change. Through their stories, you'll see how different paths to healing can be, highlighting the uniqueness of each person's experience.

Practical Examples of Boundary Setting, Communication, and Self-Care:

Within these case studies, you'll encounter practical examples of how individuals have implemented strategies for boundary setting, effective communication, and self-care. These examples showcase how healing strategies aren't abstract concepts, but rather actionable steps that can be tailored to individual circumstances.

Boundary Setting: You'll witness how individuals identified and communicated their boundaries to create healthier relationships with family members or others. These examples illustrate how setting boundaries is essential for creating emotional safety and maintaining self-respect.

Communication: The case studies reveal how individuals learned to communicate assertively and openly. These examples demonstrate how healthy communication fosters understanding, resolves conflicts, and nurtures supportive connections.

Self-Care: The case studies showcase how individuals integrated self-care practices into their lives. You'll see how self-care empowered them to prioritize their well-being, manage stress, and build emotional resilience.

Learning from Real-Life Experiences:

The case studies and practical examples offer a tangible way to learn from others' experiences. They provide inspiration, encouragement, and insights into the challenges and triumphs that come with healing from a narcissistic family dynamic.

By delving into these case studies, you'll find relatable narratives that resonate with your own journey. You'll witness the transformations that are possible when individuals make a commitment to self-discovery, growth, and healing. These real-life examples serve as beacons of hope and guidance, offering lessons that can inspire you on your path to creating a healthier, more empowered future.

Case Study 1: Emma's Journey to Self-Discovery

Background: Emma grew up in a narcissistic family where her opinions were often dismissed, and her achievements were overshadowed. She struggled with low self-esteem and self-doubt well into adulthood.

Healing Journey: Emma decided to seek therapy to address her emotional wounds. Through therapy, she discovered her strengths and developed self-compassion. With the support of her therapist, she set boundaries with her family and learned to communicate her needs assertively.

Boundary Setting: Emma's journey involved recognizing her right to establish boundaries. She communicated to her family that she needed space and time for herself, and she stood firm even when met with resistance. This led to healthier interactions and improved self-esteem.

Communication: Emma learned healthy communication techniques, enabling her to express herself without fear of judgment. She shared her feelings with her family using "I" statements, fostering understanding and mutual respect.

Self-Care: Emma embraced self-care practices such as journaling, meditation, and spending time with supportive friends. These practices nurtured her emotional well-being and empowered her to prioritize her needs.

Outcome: Over time, Emma's confidence grew, and she developed a stronger sense of self. She maintained a healthier relationship with her family while creating boundaries that protected her emotional well-being. Emma's journey illustrates how healing from a narcissistic family dynamic involves self-discovery, self-advocacy, and nurturing self-worth.

Case Study 2: Mark's Path to Empowerment

Background: Mark, the eldest sibling in a narcissistic family, often felt overshadowed by his parent's demands. He struggled with asserting himself and forming healthy relationships.

Healing Journey: Mark engaged in therapy to address his challenges. With guidance, he recognized his pattern of prioritizing others' needs over his own, which stemmed from his family role.

Boundary Setting: Mark learned to set boundaries by acknowledging his own needs and values. He communicated to his family that he needed space to pursue his goals and passions, even when faced with initial resistance.

Communication: Mark improved his communication skills, expressing his thoughts and desires openly. He confronted his family's expectations and asserted his own aspirations.

Self-Care: Mark incorporated self-care routines like exercise, reading, and pursuing hobbies he enjoyed. These activities enhanced his self-esteem and provided an outlet for stress.

Outcome: As Mark continued his healing journey, he found a renewed sense of empowerment and self-assuredness. He developed fulfilling relationships outside his family and achieved personal goals. Mark's story demonstrates how individuals can break free from limiting family roles, set boundaries, and cultivate a stronger sense of self.

Case Study 3: Sarah's Road to Inner Harmony

Background: Sarah, the scapegoat in her narcissistic family, often faced blame and criticism. She struggled with low self-esteem and feelings of isolation.

Healing Journey: Sarah engaged in therapy to address her past wounds. Through therapy, she learned to challenge her negative self-perceptions and reframe her beliefs.

Boundary Setting: Sarah recognized the importance of boundaries and communicated her limits to her family. She advocated for herself, preventing others from assigning blame unfairly.

Communication: Sarah honed her communication skills, expressing her emotions and thoughts assertively. She found her voice and confronted her family's behaviour when necessary.

Self-Care: Sarah embraced self-care rituals, including mindfulness practices and spending time in nature. These practices helped her manage anxiety and build emotional resilience.

Outcome: Over time, Sarah's self-esteem improved, and she formed healthier relationships based on mutual respect. She found a sense of belonging beyond her family unit and experienced a newfound sense of harmony within herself. Sarah's journey exemplifies how healing can lead to self-empowerment and a balanced emotional state.

Each case study illustrates the unique challenges and triumphs that come with healing from a narcissistic family dynamic. These stories showcase how individuals can implement strategies such as boundary setting, communication improvement, and self-care to foster personal growth, empowerment, and a stronger sense of self.

Chapter 10

Moving Forward and Thriving: Sustaining Your Growth

As you reach the final chapter of your healing journey, it's time to shift your focus from overcoming challenges to embracing a future filled with growth and fulfilment. In this chapter, we explore how to celebrate your progress, implement long-term strategies for ongoing development, and build a network that supports your thriving.

Celebrating Progress:

Take a moment to celebrate how far you've come. Recognize the milestones you've achieved and the internal transformations you've undergone. Celebrating progress is an acknowledgment of your resilience and a testament to your dedication to personal growth. Reflect on the positive changes you've made and the lessons you've learned from your healing journey.

Long-Term Strategies for Continued Growth:

Your healing journey is an ongoing process. To continue thriving, consider implementing long-term strategies that support your growth:

Self-Reflection: Regularly assess your emotions, thoughts, and progress. Journaling, meditation, and self-assessment exercises can help you stay connected to your evolving needs.

Learning and Development: Cultivate a curious mindset by seeking out learning opportunities. This could involve reading books, attending workshops, or engaging in activities that expand your knowledge and skills.

Setting Goals: Define short-term and long-term goals aligned with your values and aspirations. These goals provide direction and motivation for your ongoing journey.

Adaptability: Embrace change as a catalyst for growth. Be open to new experiences, challenges, and opportunities, and use them to propel your personal development.

Creating a Supportive Network:

Surround yourself with individuals who uplift and support you. Building a network of friends, mentors, and like-minded individuals provides a safety net during times of challenge and amplifies your victories:

1. **True Connections:** Cultivate relationships based on mutual respect, empathy, and authenticity. These connections offer emotional support and a sense of belonging.

2. **Mentorship:** Seek guidance from mentors who have walked similar paths. Their insights and advice can provide valuable perspectives on your journey.

3. **Collaboration:** Engage in communities that share your interests and values. These communities' foster connection and provide opportunities for collaboration and growth.

4. Thriving Beyond Healing:

The final chapter isn't the end; it's a steppingstone toward a life marked by fulfilment, purpose, and joy. Moving forward and thriving means embracing your newfound strength, self-awareness, and capacity for transformation. Your healing journey has equipped you with the tools to navigate challenges, build meaningful connections, and create a life that aligns with your true self.

As you embark on this phase of your journey, remember that healing is not a destination; it's a continuous process. Embrace every opportunity for growth, celebrate your victories, and nurture the thriving spirit within you. Your healing journey is a testament to your resilience, and your ability to move forward and thrive is a testament to your strength.

Chapter 11

Conclusion: Your Empowered Journey

As you approach the conclusion of this transformative journey, it's essential to reflect on the lessons you've learned and the growth you've achieved. The concluding chapter offers insights into how to continue embracing healing as a continuous journey and empowers you to break free from cycles that no longer serve you.

Embracing Healing as a Continuous Journey:

Healing isn't a destination; it's a lifelong journey. As you close this chapter, remember that growth, self-discovery, and transformation are ongoing processes. Continue to prioritize self-awareness, self-compassion, and self-improvement in your daily life. Embrace the fact that life is filled with ups and downs, and each experience presents an opportunity for learning and growth. By viewing healing as an ongoing journey, you empower yourself to approach challenges with resilience and open-mindedness.

Empowering Yourself to Break Cycles:

You've gained valuable insights into the dynamics of narcissistic family units and the roles they create. As you move forward, you have the power to break free from these cycles and create a new narrative for yourself:

- **Awareness:** Maintain awareness of your triggers, patterns, and behaviours that may have originated from your family dynamics. Conscious awareness empowers you to choose different responses.

- **Self-Compassion**: Be kind to yourself as you navigate challenges. Break the cycle of self-blame and self-criticism, replacing it with self-compassion and understanding.

- **Boundaries:** Continue setting and reinforcing boundaries that protect your well-being. This practice empowers you to create relationships based on mutual respect and understanding.

- **Communication**: Use your newfound communication skills to express yourself authentically and assertively. Break the cycle of silence or passive communication, fostering connections built on honesty.

Moving Forward with Empowerment:

As you close this chapter and embark on the next phase of your life, remember that you hold the keys to your own empowerment. Your healing journey has equipped you with valuable tools, insights, and strategies to create a life that aligns with your authentic self. By nurturing self-awareness, practicing self-compassion, and embracing personal growth, you can continue moving forward with confidence and empowerment.

Celebrate your progress, honour your resilience, and trust in your ability to navigate the challenges that lie ahead. As you embrace healing as a continuous journey, you empower yourself to create a life that is characterized by self-discovery, authenticity, and fulfilment. You are the author of your story, and with each new chapter, you can create a narrative that reflects your strength, resilience, and unwavering commitment to your well-being and growth.

Love & Light

Angela

Printed in Dunstable, United Kingdom